BRIGHT CAGES

BRIGHT CAGES

Selected Poems
and
Translations from the Chinese,

By Christopher Morley

Edited, with an Introduction by
Jon Bracker

UNIVERSITY OF PENNSYLVANIA PRESS
PHILADELPHIA *c 1965*

ACKNOWLEDGMENTS

The editor acknowledges his indebtedness to the following publishers and individuals for permission to reprint the poems in this volume: Mrs. Christopher Morley

J. B. Lippincott Company, for the following: "Washing the Dishes," "Pedometer," "Ars Dura," "A Grub Street Recessional"—from *Songs for a Little House* by Christopher Morley. Copyright 1917, 1945 by Christopher Morley. "When Shakespeare Laughed"—from *The Rocking Horse* by Christopher Morley. Copyright 1918, 1946 by Christopher Morley. "To His Mistress, Deploring . . . ," "Nursery Rhymes for the Tender-Hearted," "In an Auction Room," "Reciprocation," "Handicapped," "The Point of View," "Poets Easily Consoled," "An Aristocrat of the P'Un Dynasty," "Query: Who Can Alleviate . . . ," "Testament of No Sho," "The Surf"—from *Hide and Seek* by Christopher Morley. Copyright 1920, 1947 by Christopher Morley. "At the Mermaid Cafeteria," "Charles and Mary," "The Poet on the Hearth"—from *Chimneysmoke* by Christopher Morley. Copyright 1921, 1949 by Christopher Morley. "Where the Blue Begins"—from *Where the Blue Begins* by Christopher Morley. Copyright 1922, 1949 by Christopher Morley. "The Palimpsest," "Inscription for a Butterfly's Wing," "Very Few Remember," "The Hubbub of the Universe," "The Cigarette Stub," "Bivalves"—*Translations from the Chinese* by Christopher Morley. "Pragmatism," "Weakness," "Of a Child that Had Fever," "On a Portrait of Dr. Samuel Johnson, L. L. D.," "Oh, April!," "Austin Dobson," "The Epigram," "Curfew Song"—from *Parsons Pleasure* by Christopher Morley. Copyright 1923, 1950 by Christopher Morley. "Sir Kenelm to the Lady Venetia," "Chateau de Missery," "To C.H.P.," "The New Moon Feeling," "Vigillae Albae"—from *Poems* by Christopher Morley. Copyright 1927, 1954 by Christopher Morley.

"Epitaph for Love," copyright 1950 by The Saturday Review, Associates, Inc., "Atomic Fission, April 1387," copyright 1950 by The Atlantic Monthly Company, "Portrait of a Mathematician," copyright 1950 by Christopher Morley, "Preface to Bartlett," copyright 1944 by Harcourt, Brace and Company, Inc. All reprinted by permission of Doubleday & Company, Inc.

The poems from *The Middle Kingdom* by Christopher Morley, copyright, 1944, by Harcourt, Brace & World, Inc. and reprinted with their permission.

CONTENTS

II

Translations From The Chinese

... how he caught
(So charmingly, so many times)
The swift, reluctant birds of thought
In the bright cages of his rhymes.
—*Austin Dobson*

INTRODUCTION

Although well known as the author of *Parnassus on Wheels, Where the Blue Begins, Thunder on the Left,* and *Kitty Foyle,* Christopher Morley thought of himself as essentially a poet and wanted to be remembered as such. Late in his career he confided, "I have never been completely happy except when writing verse. I've the horridest feeling that after it's too late for me, someone will say, 'He wrote poetry.' " When given the opportunity in 1942 of making a selection of his writing for Whit Burnett's anthology, *This Is My Best,* Morley contributed four poems, remarking, "I hope it will not startle you if I say I think I should prefer to enter your caravan as a poet rather than in other possible disguises. . . . poetry was and remains my first love."

Morley's first book, *The Eighth Sin,* appeared in 1912 when he was twenty-two years old, and his last, *Gentlemen's Relish,* was published in 1955, two years before his death; both were volumes of verse. Enough poems for sixteen additional collections were written during a remarkably productive career. The selection of poems in *Bright Cages,* however, was made from twenty-two books, all but one of them out of print, because the best of Morley's verse spilled over into two novels, a collection of essays, and an early autobiography. Thus made available

13

for the first time is the finest poetry of Christopher Morley; readers may now sympathize with the poet's own conviction that "some of his verse is more important than has been recognized."

* * *

The opening sentence of Morley's autobiographical *John Mistletoe* is: "To be deeply rooted in a place that has meaning is perhaps the best gift a child can have." The influence of Haverford, where "Kit" Morley enjoyed the first ten years of his life, was a strong one in the formation of the poet. Today a suburb of Philadelphia, Haverford in the '90's must have been a lovely place. In the spring one can still see "the dropping flit" of the maple seeds which Morley described as "coat-hangers for a fairy's closet." Born in a house on the lawn of Haverford College, where his father taught mathematics, the young boy grew up in an arcadian setting. "How like an English nobleman's park!" was the exclamation of one British visitor. There men in white trousers played cricket on green fields, ducks swam in the pond which local children would skate on in winter, and in another area of the extensive grounds, violets showed through a coverlet of pine needles on the floor of the woods. Haverford endowed Morley with a sense of place. The Quaker institution affected him with its quiet beauty and "feeling of permanence." In the production of a poet, Morley suggested, it is helpful if he know "one coign of ground pluperfectly"; under these ideal conditions

> Her bend of soil, her smell of air
> Bottom the clearness of his mind,
> Make a deep shining there, and pass
> To inmost in, as mercury behind
> A lucid pane, makes looking glass . . .

14

Although he added that it makes little difference where this process takes place, one suspects that Morley had Haverford in mind when he wrote the lines.

At the age of nineteen, attending Haverford as a student, Morley fell in love and "reinvented the sonnet." Such attempts at verse as "To Her" and "Omnia Vincit Amor" appeared in the college magazine. "The nymphs of Bryn Mawr," Morley later stated, "are responsible for more juvenile verse in Eastern Pennsylvania than statisticians dream."

Also responsible for Morley's interest in writing poetry were two Haverford instructors. Professor of English and a specialist in the English ballad, Dr. Francis B. Gummere intoned "Lord Randall" in a voice of impressive timbre and resonance, the memory of which was to haunt Morley and would encourage him to write his "Ballad of New York, New York." With other students Morley visited in the teacher's home and sat before the fireplace over which Gummere had carved three lines by Walter Von Der Vogelweide: "Er minnet iemer deste baz/ Swer von minnen etewaz/ Hoeret singen oder lesen." Translating the lines as "Who hear something sung or read/ Of sweet love and how it sped/ Are the better lovers," Morley was to use them as his motto for *The Middle Kingdom,* a later collection of verse. Smoking a "Robin Hood" cigar—the picture of an outlaw on the band was a pleasant reminder of folk ballads—Gummere spoke to the boys about Chaucer, Milton, or perhaps of his favorites among the modern writers, Stevenson, Meredith, and Hardy. In gratitude to Gummere, who died in 1919, Morley dedicated *Gentlemen's Relish* (1955) to the teacher "born one hundred years ago and still, for his pupils, truly alive." Supplementing Gummere's influence, Dr. Albert E. Hancock, an enthusiast of Keats' poetry, introduced Morley to the poets

15

of the Romantic Period. When Morley in turn showed evidence in poetry of his own acquaintance with and interest in Shakespeare, Herrick, Pope, Wordsworth, Byron, Lamb, and their fellows, it was a way of passing on a lesson learned.

Although at Haverford Morley had been introduced to illustrious constellations of poets and had written verse of his own, he recorded in *John Mistletoe* the fact that, at the time, he and his classmates thought of literature "as something definitely Beyond the Horizon." It was not until Morley attended Oxford as a Rhodes Scholar that he came under the influence of literature as "a present living reality." There he saw Henry James and Robert Bridges receive honorary degrees, and met Sir William Osler, Sir Sidney Colvin, and Logan Pearsall Smith. "The great hall of the Examination schools was crowded to the window-sills," Morley recalled, when Belloc lectured on Rabelais; Chesterton was another favorite of the students. To read Beerbohm's Oxford farce, *Zuleika Dobson*, in its setting soon after the publication in 1911, to have John Masefield burst upon one from the pages of the *English Review*, was to learn that literature was not wholly contained within college texts.

The writers he saw and the poems he read made Morley himself eager to "lay the rhymester's switch across the rosy buttocks of the Muse," as he characteristically described the act in a poem written at the time. In years to come, critics would point to the year 1912 as the beginning of a renaissance of English poetry, but Morley maintained that at Oxford he "did not have to wait ten years to know that; I knew it then. I was sure of it: I was helping to write it."

The verses which Morley produced at Oxford were bal-

16

lades in the hearty Belloc-Chesterton manner; rondeaus and rondels inspired by his reading, in a village on the outskirts of the forest of Fontainebleau during a spring vacation, of Charles d'Orléans, Villon, and Ronsard; and parodies of Raleigh and Herrick. The titles of the poems give glimpses of the charm of Oxford student life: "Ballad of Shop-Windows in the High," "To Venus in the Ashmolean," "Mint Julep Night," and "The Passionate Student to His Junior Bursar." The poems, which show technical adroitness and felicity of phrase, as in the description of the river Isis, "through the cloth of green, stitching her silver way . . ." or the picture of a fish in a pool: "so tame he comes/ To lip your fingers offering crumbs," were, in addition, many of them, love poems with the refreshing quality of sincerity. For it was during this period that Morley met and fell earnestly in love with Helen Booth Fairchild, an American he had met in London. She was the "Only Begetter" of the poems which in the fall of 1912 were published by B. H. Blackwell as *The Eighth Sin*. The title comes from a letter by John Keats: "There is no greater sin after the seven deadly than to flatter oneself into the idea of being a great poet." Another interpretation was that of a critic in New York during the late '20's who said that the eighth sin was the price which the small bluish gray paper-covered book, of which only 250 or 300 copies had been printed, brought in the rare book market.

It would be unjust to condemn Morley's juvenilia for being no more than competent and engaging light verse not particularly different from that produced by fellow Oxford students, for the poet himself was aware of their slightness and later included only one poem from the volume in his first retrospective collection. He was to write of *The Eighth Sin*, "The perpetrator, if he thinks of it at all, thinks of it fondly as a boy's straggling nosegay, somewhat wilted in a hot eager hand, clumsily tied together with honest love."

The New York City which attracted Morley on his return from Oxford was an exciting place to seek a career. The second sight which impressed him on arrival (the first had been the starry ceiling of Grand Central Station) was the gold statue of Diana on the old Madison Square Garden, a shining silhouette against the sky; she became for Morley a symbol of this stimulating phase of his life, a symbol he used more than once in his poetry.

So recently smitten, he became enamored again, this time of a city. "A pricklejoy for poets," Morley called Manhattan, and also "the greatest unwrit poem in the world." Exploring her streets as he sought a niche in the literary world, Morley encountered for the first time the Flatiron Building, which seemed to him a ship whose prow pointed up Fifth Avenue; heard the chimes of the Metropolitan Life Insurance Building tower; and saw flocks of pigeons wheel over Madison Square. The city seemed to be growing up around him. Even at night work continued on the digging of the foundation for the Altman Building; the Empire State Building, the exposed framework on the pinnacle of which Morley was to climb as guest of the builder, was still going up.

Although his position with Doubleday, Page and Company—a "Grub Street Runner," the young factotum called himself—was at its Garden City press on Long Island, Morley lived for a number of months in the city. He was to become a suburbanite but kept in contact with city life when he returned to work at the Manhattan offices of the *New York Evening Post* and *The Saturday Review of Literature;* Morley also wrote for a while from a Nassau Street

18

hideaway which he called "the kennel." During the '40's he went three times a week to an office on West 47th Street; this sanctum, four flights up in an elevatorless building, he called "Sciatica."

One of the areas of New York which Morley came to know well was the journalistic district of Park Row. Dropping in on Don Marquis at the *Sun* offices, watching the stenographers chatting over their lunches as they sat on benches in St. Paul's burial ground, or exploring every book and cranny of an alluring side street, Morley, in William Rose Benét's description, "roved the streets with a wild paronomastic enthusiasm nothing could quell." His forays were an expression of a devotion to Manhattan which Simeon Strunsky called "one of the great love stories of history."

The details of the lifelong affair are recorded in Morley's poetry: the panorama of faces in the subway, the sounds at night of traffic in the streets, the tiny fluffs of milkweed blown into the city on an October day; these are the pictures Morley drew, partly recreated from notes taken on the spot, partly the products of happy memories. One of his longer efforts, the excellent "Ballad of New York, New York," captures much of the essence of "the Town so big men name her twice,/ Like so: N'Yawk, N'Yawk"; Morley was proud of the poem, which he worked out over a period of ten months, and believed that in it were "a few of those lightning strokes of phrase and purview that lift feet over hedges." If he had written nothing else than this poem, which is already being quoted in print and is making its way into anthologies, Christopher Morley would have earned the right to be called a poet.

In 1914 Morley married Helen Fairchild, and the young couple set up housekeeping in a little cottage on Oak

19

Avenue, Hempstead, Long Island. The domesticity which Morley enjoyed in the following years was celebrated in verses which made him a poet popular with the public. *Songs For a Little House*, the first of three collections of poetry of this period, is typical of Morley's early style. In traditional forms and with an acceptance of established poetic conventions ("For rhyme," he wrote, "is still the quiet pool/ Where Beauty is reflected,") Morley sang of the joys of married life. Soon after, with the birth of the first of his four children, he began to write poems about children and for them. There are grandparents today who quote with pleasure the opening lines of Morley's "To a Child":

> The greatest poem ever known
> Is one all poets have outgrown:
> The poetry, innate, untold,
> Of being only four years old.

And there are young men and women who recall the refrain of another of Morley's widely reprinted verses for children: "Animal crackers and cocoa to drink,/ That is the finest of suppers, I think."

It is not easy to write dispassionately of one's children, but Morley managed to do so fairly often. Even such a humble subject as a high chair, with one of his daughters in it, is transformed by Morley's skill:

> This is the battlefield that parents know
> Where one small splinter of old Adam's rib
> Withstands an entire household offering spoons.
> No use to gnash your teeth. For she will go
> Radiant to bed, glossy from crown to bib
> With milk and cereal and a surf of prunes.

The key to Morley's early popularity as a poet—and *The*

20

Rocking Horse and *Hide and Seek,* which followed *Songs For a Little House* in quick succession, met with a warm enough reception to warrant their collection, with several new poems, in *Chimneysmoke* (1921), an illustrated gift edition of the "Lyrics for Households of Two or More"— was his unabashed sentimentality. Morley felt few qualms over depicting the homelier aspects of human existence. After all, had not Herrick, Cowper, and Crabbe, all respected poets, dealt with similar subjects? "To the devil with those who pretend to ridicule sentiment," Morley declared. "There is room for enlightened sentiment, aerated by humor, stiffened with irony and self mockery, but not devoid of compassion."

Most of the early poems were written in the evenings after a day at the office. Writing with a fountain pen which he used as a staff pen, dipping it into the bottle of ink so as to have enough time to think but not so much time that he knew he was thinking, Morley might begin by putting down a phrase he had formulated on the walk home from the station or a rhyme he had found during the day. As time passed he would become too excited to sit at the desk any longer; "standing over the table leaning on elbows" was his self-description. Too absorbed to keep his pipe lit, Morley would continue to write until he became aware of the two dangers which lay in wait: the ice-box and the sofa. Cursing himself for giving in to his appetite, Morley would drink milk from a bottle the top of which, he noted approvingly, read "Grand Gorge." Then the icebox pan was emptied into the insect-loud night. Sometimes the desk to which he returned seemed "built of slippery elm, full of knots, cut in the dark while a brindle cat was mewing. There was drowsy syrup in its veins." After a short nap on the couch, the tired young writer would go off to bed for the night, although there might yet be a vault from bed at four o'clock in the morning to record a thought he did not want to lose.

The poems of this second period, it must be admitted, were written not only from the love of writing but also for the extra cash they would bring in. The expenses of a young householder were barely met by Morley's salary. As his verses were accepted by the large family magazines, he discovered that an audience for his work was growing. He began to write for this audience and produced some ephemeral verse. But if there were critics who borrowed Morley's own term, "dishpantheism," to describe what they disliked in his early verse, there were others to give him reassurance and praise. "Elinor Wylie referred to several of his lyrics as matter of which Herrick himself might be proud," reported William Rose Benét, adding that he himself felt of Morley's "In the Mermaid Cafeteria" that "Herrick did things differently, but he did no one thing any better. The elucidating phrases of this poem are remarkable. It should become a classic." It was this poem in particular that Elinor Wylie regarded so highly; Morley, apparently quite seriously, told of her offering, when she saw the lines in manuscript, any of her unpublished verses in return for the privilege of being allowed to publish the poem as her own.

In 1917 Morley moved his family to Philadelphia, where he became briefly, as he put it, "one of the little group of wilful men who edit the *Ladies' Home Journal*." The next year he was conducting a daily column for the *Philadelphia Evening Public Ledger;* there in a rolltop desk was born the first of his "translations from the Chinese," which are not translations at all, but original poems, often with an Oriental flavor, which sometimes deal with Oriental subjects. First, as "Synthetic Poems," they were Morley's mild burlesque of the then new imagism. But Morley "also had a feeling that free verse, then mainly employed as the vehicle of a rather gaudy impressionism or of mere eccentricity, might prove a viable medium for humorous, ironic, and satiric brevities. . . ."

The Oriental aspect was added to the "translations" after Morley read in the fall of 1918 the just-published first of Arthur Waley's important translations, *170 Chinese Poems*, and learned "that the ancient Chinese poets themselves were both wise and humorous." Enjoying a vogue in America, Oriental verse influenced poets whose work was known to Morley: Witter Bynner (*The Beloved Stranger*, 1919) and Amy Lowell (*Fir-Flower Tablets*, 1921). *A History of Japanese Poetry* by Curtis Hidden Page—the recipient of Morley's poem entitled "To C.H.P."—was published in 1923. "To paraphrase the old English song," Morley wrote, "it was 'Loud sing Hokku' all across the map."

Returning to the New York scene in 1920, Morley found "a landscape bizarre enough to move him deeply" and the first of the poems actually printed as "translations from the Chinese" appeared. In the beginning the verses were attributed to such pseudo-poets as "No Sho," "O B'Oi," "Po Lil Chile," and "P'Ur Fish," but, as their creator later described the process, "little by little my Chinese sages began to coalesce and assume a voice of their own. I became not their creator but their stenographer. I began to feel a certain respect and affection for the 'Old Mandarin' who was dimly emerging as their Oriental spokesman. I began to realize that the mind speaks many languages, and some of its sudden intuitions and exclamations are truly as enigmatic to us as Chinese writing. . . ." As the "Old Mandarin" took shape, Morley's verses became more poetic. Their creator no longer felt a need to apologize humorously for his lack of knowledge of Chinese, based largely as it was on the reading of laundry slips, which caused him when in doubt as to the exact meaning of a phrase always to translate it as "a bowl of jade filled with the milk of moonlight."

Although Morley thought of the "translations" as a whole as essentially American in tone, it is interesting to consider the comments of Pearl Buck, whose qualifications as an American novelist of Chinese life make her a critic worth listening to. She wrote to Morley in 1932:

> Of course, as you know, I have considered your poems in the mandarin mood quite matchless, and I have never understood how it was an American or even an Occidental could write them. After I met you, however, I divined in you a certain quality of the mandarin, and then came to the conclusion that either you had once been a mandarin in some previous life, or that the mandarin quality, which I consider invaluable because it is both precious and rare, is more universal than I thought. The explanation depends on whether one is Oriental or Occidental at bottom; you may choose the one you like better.

There is a universal quality to the "translations," yet it is also true that, in the later poems, the "Old Mandarin" came to sound a great deal like Morley, or the "Old Man" as he was known to family and intimate friends. Indeed, Louis Greenfield, Morley's office manager for a number of years, writes that the poet was actually called the "Old Mandarin" by close associates; in any case, both the fictional character and his creator were occasionally referred to by the abbreviation "O.M."

Morley had hoped that someday the "translations," which appeared over a period of thirty-five years and were

24

sometimes published along with his regular poems, might be separately collected; the best of them appear together in *Bright Cages* in a division of their own. Now one can see why as early as 1927 Leonard Bacon, the distinguished writer of light verse, claimed that "if Mr. Morley had never done anything other than *Translations From the Chinese* he would still be a notable figure. . . . Few poets restore more generously the mystery that our own clumsy hands have rubbed from the butterfly wings of the familiar."

In 1920 Morley moved his family to a large house in Roslyn, Long Island; he called the rambling structure "Green Escape" and lived there until his death thirty-seven years later. Soon after the move, a change could be perceived in Morley's writings. He became less the journalist—for he had produced many essays and much popular fiction since his return from Oxford—and more the creative writer, less the versifier and more the poet. It was the writing, in 1921, of an unmarketable short story, "Referred to the Author," Morley maintained, that marked the dividing line if one were to be drawn. The next year saw the publication of his first important novel, the allegorical *Where the Blue Begins,* which was prefaced with a lyric in which Morley expressed his determination to break through the elements which held him pent and to "make his furious sonnet." More and more he wanted to be able to give up the hack work which had been necessary, and to get on to the projects which could engage his heart as well as his head. The little collection of fervently philosophical essays, *Inward Ho!,* which came out in 1923, further indicated Morley's new and serious concerns. In 1923 also he left the *New York Evening Post,* for which he had conducted a weekly column for three years. The poem "Grub Street Recessional" is Morley's verse farewell to the newspaper world, as *Religio Journalistici* (1924) is his prose goodbye. Although that year he became a contributing editor of *The Saturday Review of Literature* and wrote for the magazine once a week for fourteen years, Morley now only commuted to Manhattan for part of the week and was able to do a portion of his writing at home. As the sale of his prose works increased and his reputation grew, Morley became financially somewhat less dependent on pleasing an audience, particularly in poetry, which he wrote now more from private desire than public demand.

Suburban life agreed with him. The village where William Cullen Bryant had lived was a small community when Morley arrived; as a matter of fact, the first kerosene lamps were installed because he complained of bumping into a cow one night on the walk home from the station. Morley saw Roslyn grow and did not hold aloof from its life but weeded beets in the community garden during World War II and successfully campaigned against the renovation of the fascinatingly grotesque old Long Island Railroad station-house. A familiar figure in his worn blue sweater and comfortable trousers, he could be seen walking with his beloved spaniel, Corky, along the winding roads of Roslyn Estates; in his hip pocket a memorandum book "caressed the natural curvature."

In the summer Morley liked to clip the lawn with the office shears with which he had compiled several collections of essays. In the fall he raked and burned leaves and chopped wood for the furnace; when it became too cold to write in "the Knothole," the log cabin on an adjoining wood-lot, Morley retreated to the house where he had a study bursting with books and papers, on the shelves, tables, the floor, and even, for a while, on an ironing board. In the spring he observed how the white propellors of the backyard dogwood tree spun in the breeze; at night Orion stalked the sky while in the rose bushes fireflies "morsed about."

Life in Roslyn not only gave Morley material for a number of his finest poems, but also provided the setting for his last novel, the partially autobiographical *The Man Who Made Friends With Himself*. Richard Tolman, a literary agent who is the main character of the novel, expresses in verse his and Morley's enthusiasm for existence:

> The least last latest trivial thing
> Is what empowers me to sing:
> The labile sweetness of the rose,
> Or peonies, pepper to the nose;
> How, on your memory, imprint
> The sharpness of my backyard mint?

This was the problem that Morley set himself to solve: the communication of universal sensations. In *John Mistletoe* he had said:

> One of the things I shall miss most when I am dead
> Will be walking with naked feet on bare floors
> In summer nights, when the hardwood boards
> Are deliciously tepid to the palms of the feet.
> For if you love life you should love it all over
> And even feet have their privileges.

Knowing that after he was gone no one would notice things just as he had, Morley left us in poetry a legacy of his loves.

It is tempting to try to divide a man's career into neat compartments, each one exhibiting greater virtues until one can crown the person an indisputably major figure. "Juvenilia" is the easiest label to make stick, and "early work" is not hard to apply, but after that the going gets rougher and the man's writing will not always fall into three groups to be called "mature," "more mature," and "most mature." Having said this, one still feels that in the case of Morley the publication of the large retrospective collected *Poems* of 1929 marks a division worth noting. In the volume Morley collected all of the poetry he wished to preserve; he omitted all of *The Eighth Sin* and a number of poems from the other early volumes. A few new poems, among them two charming lyrics, were added.

Included in the *Poems* was the unusual long poem, *Toulemonde*, which had been published separately the previous year. In this work Morley took as his theme the meaning of a man's life; it was a theme he was to return to more than once, and particularly in the adventures of Richard Tolman, whose name is an adaptation of "Toulemonde," or "everybody." The form, however, of blank verse varied with interludes of song, was not entirely successful and although Morley felt a strong affection for the poem and returned to the theme in later shorter "Toulemonde" poems, most reviewers agreed that the volume was not one of his best.

If during the early '20's Morley showed an increased concentration on the problems of the art of writing, he was faced in the early '30's—his forties—with problems in the art of living. His recent two year fling at play producing in Hoboken had ended in financial difficulties and the shock of discovering the dishonesty of a trusted associate. Morley began to take stock of himself and the more bohemian aspects of his theatrical experience lost some of their allure. He had a "concern"—in the Quaker sense— to tell of an examined life and did so in *John Mistletoe*, his reflective, poetic autobiography, which was published in 1931. Succeeding years showed a somewhat mellowed man.

After the juvenilia of 1912 and the early celebrations of domesticity of 1914-29, a third period of Morley's verse is represented in *The Middle Kingdom, Spirit Level, Poetry Package,* and *The Ballad of New York, New York, and Other Poems;* the poems in these collections were written in the years 1929-50. In them Morley's individual voice is heard more clearly than in preceding collections. Here are the poetic milestones of the passage of time. One of the most successful is "Ammonoosuc," a ballad which describes a deeply felt experience in Morley's life, a return to nature which rejuvenated the poet and committed him to rededication. Of the poem William Rose Benét wrote, "Emerson is one of my gods as a poet, and I get the same feeling when I read:

> Where her crystal overran it
> I lay down in channeled granite;
> Braced against the pushing planet
> I bathed in Ammonoosuc.

The last two lines Emerson would have wished to write." Another moving experience, the marriage of his daughter Louise, is the subject of "For a Daughter's Wedding." Also among the poems of this period is the tender description of Morley's fifteen year-old spaniel, through which Corky may well join the company of Cowper's Beau and Elizabeth Barrett Browning's Flush. Realizing that he, too, was advancing in years, Morley wrote his fortunately premature "Nightsong of Lord Culverin on the Drawbridge of Castle Querulous," the lovely last lines of which call for no editorial comment:

> Soft airs, wing-beetles, crowd about!
> Good night, my lovers. My lamp is out.

29

Some of the best poems of Morley's middle period appeared in *Poetry Package*, a book which has a curious publishing history. Thirty-six years earlier Morley had bought a magazine on the train which brought him to New York City; in it an advertisement for William Rose Benét's *Merchants From Cathay* caught his eye. "Would it ever be possible," he mused, "for me also to get some poems printed, and even maybe to meet, just once and a while, men of printed poems and musical names . . ." Morley and Benét did meet and become close friends in the early '20's. Now, in 1949, another advertisement caught Morley's eye. A large New York department store was offering, among other books in a "Sale of the Unsalable," a book of poems by Benét and one by himself together as a "Poetry Package" for a dollar. At Morley's suggestion, then, the two poets selected the best poems from among their most recent and had them published by Louis Greenfield in an attractive paperbound volume. The co-authors of *Poetry Package* were only identified by their initials on the cover and title page; inside, the poems were attributed to "D.D." and "P.C.," which only initiates would recognize as "Dove Dulcet" and "Pigeon Cove," pseudonyms under which Morley and Benét, respectively, had published verse. The introduction, signed only "Cuckoo," was actually by the respected critic Chauncey Brewster Tinker; the motif was further carried out by a cover caricature of the poets as birds, Benét a pigeon operating a typewriter with one toe, and Morley a bearded and bespectacled dove writing with a quill pen. When the book came out, Morley told an interviewer that it had been published in memory of another collaboration, the *Lyrical Ballads* of Wordsworth and Coleridge.

Like Thomas Hardy, whose poetry he admired, Morley

wrote some of his finest poems toward the end of a long writing career. Writing of Hardy, Morley could have been speaking of himself:

> Someone is sure to reiterate the old legend that it was pique or deep indignation at fool criticisms that turned Hardy from the novel to poetry. That seems to me inconceivable. A man of his vitality and toughness writes as and how he pleases; and the sequence of a man's work obeys laws deeper than publicity. He turned to poetry, one may guess, because he could better express in that measure what he wanted to say.

After completing *The Man Who Made Friends With Himself,* Morley wrote to friends that "I have a sudden horrid feeling, probably glandular, that I am grown up; therefore I now devote myself to the only perfect excitement I have ever had, writing verse." He was not displeased with past performances and for Christmas, 1951, sent to friends a privately printed pamphlet, *A Pride of Sonnets,* which contained nineteen previously published poems. Among them was the charming "Charles and Mary," which Walter De La Mare had chosen as one of twenty-four sonnets, some of them by such masters as Shelley, Keats, and Wordsworth, for "Sweet as Roses, A Little Treasury of Sonnets," which appeared in *The Saturday Book* for 1950. The sonnet form was a favorite of Morley's; his success with the conventional structure is shown in the sixteen examples in *Bright Cages.*

The fourth and final division in Morley's career as a poet is that of the poems produced after a stroke suffered in 1951 temporarily paralyzed his right arm and hand. Painfully he taught himself to type again (Morley had given up writing with a fountain pen in the late '30's, in an attempt to simplify his style). In his slow recovery from

31

illness, Morley discovered that "when a word makes its way safely and scribably from skull to fingers . . . I probably really mean or want it." Enough poems were written for a final collection, *Gentlemen's Relish,* before a second stroke two years before his death in 1957 made both speech and writing impossible.

The approach of death can be seen in several poems in the volume, but the book itself is full of life. "Elected Silence: Three Sonnets," for example, in which Morley pays tribute to the memory of William Rose Benét, who had died in 1950, is refreshingly free from elegiac formality. Another individual treatment of the theme of death is the witty "Morning After," in which, asked by St. Peter what he would most enjoy in Heaven, the poet answers: "To learn again how words, well shuffled,/ Can sort miraculously into rhyme;/ Or better still, read as for the first time/ One of the Adventures of Sherlock Holmes." Morley thought of himself, with some reason, as a forgotten man in his last years, but the once popular poet was not bitter towards a fickle public. He felt that he had written well and was content. As he expressed it in verse:

> All passion spent, and all publicity,
> My telephone not numbered in the book,
> Nowhere will you find a happier man.
> All birds are redbreast in the setting sun.

❋   ❋   ❋

As to the technical aspects of the poetry, one wonders just what service would be performed the reader were we to approach Morley's verse with the various tools of the critic—to count the number of syllables and ascertain the stresses, noting the sequence of feminine and masculine rhymes both internal and external, carefully paying attention to the distinctions between a rondeau and a rondel, a ballad and a ballade, and finally to correctly label the various specimens like so many butterflies preserved in an exhibit case. It is well, perhaps, to note that Morley successfully essayed a number of complicated French verse forms in addition to being adept at the more usual English ones, to remark that on occasion he wrote *vers libre* but that, except for the "translations from the Chinese," he was basically an old-fashioned poet for whom rhyme was important. If one were to read some of Morley's favorite poets—Austin Dobson, Sir William Watson, and Robert Louis Stevenson, as well as Keats, Shelley, and Wordsworth—one might better assess what he attempted, but it may well be better simply to read and enjoy each poem separately.

One thinks wryly of the teacher who told his students, "Go home and appreciate these poems by Monday." But even such a respected writer as T. S. Eliot has defined the critic he was most grateful to as "the one who can make me look at something I have never looked at before, or looked at only with eyes clouded by prejudice, set me face to face with it, and then leave me alone with it. From that point, I must rely upon my own sensibility, intelligence and capacity for wisdom."

Perhaps the editor might remark that the "Wooing Song for Sir Toby" was written to supplement the action of Shakespeare's *Twelfth Night,* in which Morley felt that Sir Toby and Maria marry too precipitately; it may be helpful for the reader to know, too, that the Sir Kenelm mentioned in the poems is Sir Kenelm Digby, the seventeenth century English naval commander, diplomat, and author. Further interest may be derived from the poems if one is reminded, when reading "Oh To Be In 'Bartlett'

Now That April's Here," that Morley edited two versions of *Familiar Quotations;* when reading "Portrait of a Mathematician," that Morley's father was a noted geometer; and that the Chateau de Missery of the poem was an estate on the Cote d'Or at which Morley was once a guest. But basically such information is small beer; if the lines are good it cannot make them better and if they are bad, it cannot help at all. Morley's poetry, it need only be noted, exhibits symbolism without recourse to private mythology, knowledge without offensive pedantry, and complexity with neither wilful obscurity nor any of the seven types of ambiguity discovered by William Empson and embraced so ardently by the gradgrind mind. No, Christopher Morley's poetry is too honest and too human and communicates too directly with the reader for an explicator to feel very much at home. As Morley's "Old Mandarin" put it:

> I am weary
> Of critical theory.
>
> I'm empiric
> About a lyric.
>
> Either it sings
> Like a happy peasant,
> Or—one of those things—
> It just doesn't.

In the opinion of the editor, the poems which follow sing.

I

POEMS

IN A SECOND-HAND BOOKSHOP

What waits me on these shelves? I cannot guess,
But feel the sure foreboding; there will cry
A voice of human laughter or distress,
A word that no one needs as much as I.

For always where old books are sold and bought
There comes that twinge of dreadful subtlety—
These words were actual, and they were thought
By someone who was once alive, like me.

TWILIGHT

Someone has lit the lamp, and hung
The house with curtains of cool blue,
Someone (I cannot tell you who)
Has put bright candles all among
Our empty rooms. Since we are young
For keeping house, and only two,
Someone has lit the lamp, and hung
The house with curtains of cool blue.
Our lamp, the moon so deftly swung
Aloft; the stars our candles new;
Our housekeeper? I have no clue.
I only know what I have sung—
Someone has lit the lamp, and hung
The house with curtains of cool blue.

WASHING THE DISHES

When we on simple rations sup
How easy is the washing up!
But heavy feeding complicates
The task by soiling many plates.

And though I grant that I have prayed
That we might find a serving-maid,
I'd scullion all my days, I think,
To see Her smile across the sink!

I wash, She wipes. In water hot
I souse each dish and pan and pot;
While Taffy mutters, purrs, and begs,
And rubs himself against my legs.

The man who never in his life
Has washed the dishes with his wife
Or polished up the silver plate—
He still is largely celibate.

One warning: there is certain ware
That must be handled with all care:
The Lord Himself will give you up
If you should drop a willow cup!

NURSERY RHYMES FOR THE
TENDER-HEARTED

(Dedicated to Don Marquis)

I

Scuttle, scuttle, little roach—
How you run when I approach:
Up above the pantry shelf,
Hastening to secrete yourself.

Most adventurous of vermin,
How I wish I could determine
How you spend your hours of ease,
Perhaps reclining on the cheese.

Cook has gone, and all is dark—
Then the kitchen is your park:
In the garbage heap that she leaves
Do you browse among the tea leaves?

How delightful to suspect
All the places you have trekked:
Does your long antenna whisk its
Gentle tip across the biscuits?

Do you linger, little soul,
Drowsing in our sugar bowl?
Or, abandonment most utter,
Shake a shimmy on the butter?

39

Do you chant your simple tunes
Swimming in the baby's prunes?
Then, when dawn comes, do you slink
Homeward to the kitchen sink?

Timid roach, why be so shy?
We are brothers, thou and I.
In the midnight, like yourself,
I explore the pantry shelf!

OF A CHILD THAT HAD FEVER

I bid you, mock not Eros
    Lest Eros mock with you.
His is a hot distemper
    That hath no feverfew.

Love, like a child in sickness,
    Brilliant, languid, still,
In fiery weakness lying,
    Accepts, and hath no will.

See, in that warm dispassion,
    Less grievance than surprise,
And pitiable brightness
    In his poor wondering eyes.

Oh delicate heat and madness,
    Oh lust unnerved and faint:

Sparkling in veins and fibres,
    Division and attaint!

I bid you, mock not Eros;
    He knows not doubt or shame,
And, unaware of proverbs,
    The burnt child craves the flame.

A SONG FOR EROS

If, in days of sullen air,
    Dark with anger, dull with grief,
Merciful and unaware
    There transpire for thy relief
        Lighter mood or cleaner sky—
        Look no further: it is I.

Bandaged close and held apart
    Are thy mortal wounds that bleed,
Yet some subtle healer's art
    Touches on thy secret need:
        What physician, then, to bless?
        It was I, eased thy distress.

Beauty never guessed before
    Universal to the gaze:
Laughter copious to restore
    All the waste of barren days:
        Cistern water turned to wine—
        Yea, these miracles are mine.

41

Under Zeus' immortal nod
  I am passion undefiled:
I, the child that is a god
    And the god that is a child.
      Canst thou not identify
      Thy magician? It is I.

DICHOTOMY

I saw no merit in the scheme
  Of Nature's primitive division:
Though sex, they told me, was supreme,
  I held it always in suspicion:
    It seemed too gross, too much imbued
    With propagative purpose crude.

But now, O palinode, confess:
  Dichotomy proves more appealing,
For since I saw you, loveliness,
  I have a wholly different feeling:
    To my astonishment intense,
    Biology makes better sense.

Magnificent is Nature's plan,
  Provocative, ingenious very,
To make a woman and a man
  So mutually necessary:
    Let Beauty flourish her allures—
    I am, appetitively yours. . . .

42

DOGWOOD TREE

Whiteness crept up through the woody veins
    And spread all sudden on the unknowing air—
That should have cured stupidities and pains?
    I could not watch it long. It's rude to stare.

And you made nothing of it, ere it vanished?
    That naked beauty of your own dear Day,
Life's whitest body—
    I was grateful and astonished,
But what was there to say?

A toss of foaming like the crystal shatter
    Of a bursting wave, in magic pause—
And was that all you thought about the matter?
    I wanted to tell *you* how beautiful it was.

EPITAPH FOR LOVE

(Res plena timoris amor—Ovid)

Love is a timid anxious thing
    That does not say itself with ease,
Belatedly remembering
    Its rituals were these:

The body's goodness, bone-and-breech;
    Absurdity, so sweet to share;
And, third of all, to learn or teach,
    The plain prosaics of despair.

Love is embarrassed to have known
    So much that never can be said,
Aware how helpless and alone
    The flesh is when we're dead:
Then godlike in our coarse abode
    Resents to let the mercy go—
Who else, in comic mortal mode
    Will cherish earth and bless it so?

Love—and how many shades of it,
    More than the elder statesmen guess—
Has many curious kinds of wit,
    Says No as well as Yes.
The show ends? As the curtains close
    Be this Love's epitaph and heart:—
I gave no countenance to those
    Who plan to tear the world apart.

YOUNG AMHERST'S MADRIGAL

(For Jocunda Vassar)

Such strong silence I had learned,
    When to cloak, when to dissemble
Passionate desires that burned,
    Lonely nights that made me tremble.

So, accustomed to disguise,
    Taught by distance and transgression,
When at last I met your eyes
    I spoke still with some discretion.

Then the sudden triumph grew:
    I by merriment was chidden—
I don't need to hide from you
    Thoughts that just for you were hidden.

A MOTHER'S DAY POEM IN MEMORY OF MY MOTHER, WHO CARED VERY LITTLE FOR MOTHER'S DAY

My mother (and God rest her gallant soul)
    Dictated me a prayer when I was young:
"Pray the Lord to help you to control
    Your temper, your excitement, and your tongue."

That petition, at my mother's knee,
Was, I hope, good discipline for me—
And yet I've rarely known full ecstasy
    Except when I have let them rip, all three.

PORTRAIT OF A MATHEMATICIAN

Sweep the pale hair, like wings, above the ears;
    Whittle the nose, and carve and bone the jaw;
Blank the studying eyes, till human fears
    Eliminate in universal law.

Slack the mortal shirt, stiffen the hands,
　　Holding the dear old pipe, half-smoked, unlit—
So, lovingly, we loose Orion's Bands
　　And write equation with the Infinite.

WHERE THE BLUE BEGINS

　　I am not free—
　　And it may be
Life is too tight around my shins;
　　For, unlike you,
　　I can't break through,
A truant where the blue begins.

　　Out of the very element
　　Of bondage, that here holds me pent,
I'll make my furious sonnet:
　　I'll turn my noose
　　To tight-rope use
And madly dance upon it.

　　So I will take
　　My leash, and make
A wilder and more subtle fleeing—
　　And I shall be
　　More escapading and more free
Than you have ever dreamed of being!

DUSK IN THE NORTH WING OF A COLLEGE LIBRARY

Swift as the twilight bird
 Tunnels in privet blossom,
Straight as the homesick word
 Into the middle bosom,

These, unerring, steered
 Weaving the sweethour's music;
Words and wings endeared
 Became the English Basic.

Trill the lawnmower snores,
 Lazy the sunlight westers
Slow as cricketing scores
 In Hampshires or in Leicesters—

But all I only crave
 When greens are shadow-slanted
Is talk beyond the grave,
 Unearthly and enchanted.

I have abandoned me,
 But here, in printed musk
Unblemished prosody
 Divisioned in the dusk.

CURFEW SONG

(To an old Burgundian music)

Candle-flame leans toward the chimney
    And the hearthfire toward the star—
Every fiery bit of burning
    Yearns where greater blazes are.
Yet must every shining ember
Sparkling high or low, remember
All that's tinder comes to cinder,
    Yellow suns burn through and char—
Lights of earth, Oh be not fretful:
Only ask that sweet forgetful
    Darkness fold us, near and far.

Dowse the taper softly, softly
    Lest the little flame take fright—
Crown him with this cap of folly,
    Dancing clown of candle-light.
Now let every weary spirit
Warmth of bed and sleep inherit
And in drowsing think of rousing
    To a morning calm and bright—
Thankful for the perfect blessing
Of a future there's no guessing:
    So, Messieurs, Mesdames—Good-Night!

COCKCROW IN SPRING

At midnight, in a sickbed world,
    The yard still grimed with snow,
He arched his fated throat, and skirled,
    And let his challenge go.
      And still the cock doth crow.

The oldest cry above the sod
    When dung and crocus blow:
The voice of the unconscious god
    That bids men dig and sow.
      And still the cock doth crow.

O bend the note, heraldic bird,
    Like arrow from the bow;
The sharpest clarion ever heard
    To let the jaded know
      That still the cock doth crow.

Before centurions cast the dice
    To pawnbroke friend and foe,
Or earth make her denial thrice,
    Sing, chanticleer, what ho!
      And still the cock doth crow.

WINTER MOON

In the clear inkwell of tonight,
Embayed in rolling silver scud,
A floating Athens, marble-bright,
Rules the republics of the blood.

Beshrew her then! So say we all
Who perish in our septuagint:
Permit one mortal caterwaul,
One molten stick of human print.

Scotch-granite as the Stone of Scoon,
Numb State Department in the sky,
Barren with protocol—Oh Moon,
One final toast, before we die:—

Never creator, mere consumer,
The moon, who has no sense of humor.

FROGS AND SQUIRRELS

The moon is not so far away
    Above my favorite crooked tree,
Where greenbud-hungry squirrels sway
    In empty April tracery.

The frogs, in my mudhumble swamp,
    Are whistlingales of boyhood joy;
But squirrels only grind and chomp,
    And care not how much they destroy.

As Keats once said, in a wonderful letter,
I've written a poem . . . I feel better.

PORPOISES

Offshore my seaside beach
    A file of porpoise grunt like dogs;
Ratchet backs, each after each,
    Roll like a wheel of cogs,
    Like the rim with teeth
    Of a great gear beneath.

Each smoothly slipping dorsal
    Turns momentous ocean on his fins:
Proxy for the Wheelwright Universal
    I applaud; but my head spins.

Then porpoise, when he wearies
Of playing shove in series
    Slips from the chain of push
    And wheeling free
    Spouts, snorts, and wallows flush
    Rotarian of the sea.

CATS

How intelligent are cats
How dignified and how congenial:
They never cry "Hang onto your hats!"
    They do not worry,
    They are not menial.

Swift without hurry,
Soft and furry
    And full of grace
Pointed ear and petal toe
Uncommunicative go:
The more they know
The more they show
    A Buddha face.

For what they want, they make a bee-line
And call it feline.
They roll and stretch, and so their figure
Does not grow bigger.
With milk and salmon mixed with Wheaties
They avoid diabetes.

In the country or the city,
Whether in houses or in flats,
By open fires or thermostats,
Some people have allergies from cats—
What a pity!

UP TAILS ALL

How does a dog's tail feel
In woe or weal?
I love to think:
What makes it curl like orange peel?
What makes it sink?

Stumps
Chopped close to rumps
Can show the dumps
But
The eloquent mutt
With tail uncut,
The natural pooch,
Feels joy from brain to gristle
Like a shot of hooch.
If he were a boy he'd whistle.

He's all agog
At being a dog.

OF AN ANCIENT SPANIEL IN HER
FIFTEENTH YEAR

She was never a dog that had much sense,
Too excitable, too intense,
But she had the cocker's gift of charm.
She never knew what to do with a bone,
But shielded all her life from harm
She cost me several years of my own.

Sweet old pooch! These final years
She rubs white chaps and floating ears
In summersweet suburban loam;
Digs, she thinks, a final home:
Scoops every day fresh graves to lie,
Humble and contented, knowing
Where, any day now, she'll be going—
And so do I.

I said, buying with Christmas care,
Her collar and tag for '49:
This is the last she'll ever wear
(And the same is true of mine).
Equal mercy, and equal dark
Await us both, eternally,
But I was always ready to bark—
And so was she.

TO HIS MISTRESS, DEPLORING THAT
HE IS NOT AN ELIZABETHAN GALAXY

Why did not Fate to me bequeath an
Utterance Elizabethan?

It would have been delight to me
If *natus ante* 1603.

My stuff would not be soon forgotten
If I could write like Harry Wotton.

I wish that I could wield the pen
Like William Drummond of Hawthornden.

I would not fear the ticking clock
If I were Browne of Tavistock.

For blithe conceits I would not worry
If I were Raleigh, or the Earl of Surrey.

I wish (I hope I am not silly?)
That I could juggle words like Lyly.

I envy many a lyric champion,
I.e., viz., e.g., Thomas Campion.

I creak my rhymes up like a derrick,
I ne'er will be a Robin Herrick.

My wits are dull as an old Barlow—
I wish that I were Christopher Marlowe.

In short, I'd like to be Philip Sidney,
Or some one else of that same kidney.

For if I were, my lady's looks
    And all my lyric special pleading
Would be in all the future books,
    And called, at college, *Required Reading*.

WOOING SONG FOR SIR TOBY

When Phyllis laid her smock to bleach
    Along the hawthorne prickle,
Her senseless linen soon did teach
    My fancy how to tickle;
Then first methought what pretty charms
    That shift would be enfolding—
Ah, better for a shepherd's arms
    To have such jocund holding:
        In every tree the birds cry, Doxy,
        Love was never done by proxy.

The empty wind that puffs her weed
    Is too indifferent squiring;
More corporal is maidens' need
    To tumble their attiring.
The cuckoo tells his leman's clock
    And summer's getting weather—
Ah, speed the day when shirt and smock
    Lie on the hedge together:
        In every tree the birds cry, Doxy,
        Love was never done by proxy.

SIR KENELM TO THE LADY VENETIA

(1624)

Hold high your gallant head
    Because I love you:
But nothing, when we're dead,
    Can I have of you.

So with my wholesome lust
    I will acquaint you
And with what words I must
    My picture paint you:

My folly—and my wit
    That marked and found you,
My arms that quaintly fit
    When they're around you.

Dear trouble, dark delight
    Since first I met you—
Oh now, for peace to-night
    Let me forget you.

No woman ever bred
    Can rise above you:
Hold high your gallant head
    Because I love you!

OH, APRIL!

Oh, April, April, April,
Sweet song-enchanted word!
When March went out at midnight
Each sleeping poet stirred—
From Hanover to Hatteras
Each poet on his mattress
Was whispering unheard:
    Daffodill and *thrill* and *spill*,
    Hill, will, still, and *windowsill*—
Darling poets, hark, oh, hark,
Softly rhyming in the dark!

When April comes, each poet
With secret glory glows—
Instinctively he knows it,
And to his art he owes it
Oh, April, April, April,
In mere mechanic prose:
    The Muse, that has been truant,
    Is suddenly more fluent
(As this impromptu shows).

No longer to enclose it
How sweet for either sex
When even minor poets
Are cashing minor checks.

In April, April, April,
    Sing *tree* and *free* and *sea*—
But, ah, no April demiurge
    Shall make a Fool of me!

WHILE REVISING SOME VERSES

Here, in a sky so pure, weather so sweet
How can a verse endure
Fit to compete?
These were my love of earth, truly confessed:
Broken the word comes forth.
Silence was best.

Song that eluded print, pen still unwet,
Letter that was not sent,
Type never set:
Those, in the hidden wit, nothing can fret.
Silence is exquisite—
And yet . . . and yet . . .

VIII

No bird has built an April nest
    More instinctive than my rhyme,
A hidden coil where thought can rest
    In lonely or in stormy time.

I weave for you these twigs and straws,
  The casual shreds of every day:
Your love can shelter there for pause
  And, when it needs to, fly away.

I build it hidden, shy, unknown,
  And weatherwise, with simple care.
And even when the bird has flown
  The empty nest will still be there.

THE POET ON THE HEARTH

When fire is kindled on the dogs,
  But still the stubborn oak delays,
Small embers laid above the logs
  Will draw them into sudden blaze.

Just so the minor poet's part:
  (A greater he need not desire)
The charcoal of his burning heart
  May light some Master into fire!

THE EPIGRAM

To write an epic or a novel
  Seems straightforward work to me—
By conscientious indentation
  The beaver bevels down the tree;

But, with the imprecisive arrow
 The intended acorn fairly struck—
Such is epigram, requiring
 Wit, occasion, and good luck!

AT THE MERMAID CAFETERIA

Truth is enough for prose:
Calmly it goes
To tell just what it knows.

For verse, skill will suffice—
Delicate, nice
Casting of verbal dice.

Poetry, men attain
By subtler pain
More flagrant in the brain—

An honesty unfeigned,
A heart unchained,
A madness well restrained.

IVORY PENTHOUSE

If he could have his druthers
 Every poet knows
He would avoid the bothers
 Of writing careful prose.

For in his verse he gathers
     Such music, such finesse,
Unwrung remain his withers
     If it never goes to press.

O secret poets, brothers!
     Ourselves rereading still—
We know how few, few others
     Ever will.

A GRUB STREET RECESSIONAL

O noble gracious English tongue
Whose fibres we so sadly twist,
For caitiff measures he has sung
Have pardon on the journalist.

For mumbled metre, leaden pun,
For slipshod rhyme, and lazy word,
Have pity on this graceless one—
Thy mercy on Thy servant, Lord!

The metaphors and tropes depart,
Our little clippings fade and bleach:
There is no virtue and no art
Save in straightforward Saxon speech.

Yet not in ignorance or spite,
Nor with Thy noble past forgot
We sinned: indeed we had to write
To keep a fire beneath the pot.

62

Then grant that in the coming time,
With inky hand and polished sleeve,
In lucid prose or honest rhyme
Some worthy task we may achieve—

Some pinnacled and marbled phrase,
Some lyric, breaking like the sea,
That we may learn, not hoping praise,
The gift of Thy simplicity.

FOREVER AMBROSIA

(Odyssey, Book V.)

Calypso
Is a bit of a dipso,
She can't keep up her pants, they slip so.

She always telegraphs her punches
By serving those ambrosial lunches.

And after getting Ulysses blotto
Leads him to her private grotto.

The Ancient Mariner tires of nectar
Had without benefit of rector,

And hankering to hoist Blue Peter
Gets so he's afraid to meet her.

After seven years, one afternoon
She says: "You're not *going*? What, so soon?"

Sadly the hero reaffirms:
"I can't be immortal on your terms.

"No can do. Even in a cave
I'm too pooped to misbehave.

"Listen, lady, it simply shows ya
Men can't live just on ambrosia."

Calypso laughed and laughed and laughed.
"Okay; I'll help you build a raft."

ATOMIC FISSION, APRIL 1387

Whan that Aprille, douce and pluviale . . .

Hand halted. Ink was pending in the fork
Where two tongues divided, equal twins.
Down the hairline of the slitten quill
Language in poise.

            He looked outdoors
On Kentish spring—fresh as a *marguerite*?
Fresh as a *day's eye* we say in Our Town?

The barnyard pinion dipped deep in the horn,
Struck, and rewrote:
Whan that Aprille with his shoures soote. . . .

English was born.

WHEN SHAKESPEARE LAUGHED

When Shakespeare laughed, the fun began!
Even the tavern barmaids ran
    To choke in secret, and unbent
    A lace, to ease their merriment.
The *Mermaid* rocked to hear the man.

Then Ben his aching girth would span,
And roar above the pasty pan,
    "Avast thee, Will, for I am spent!"
    When Shakespeare laughed.

I' faith, let him be grave who can
When Falstaff, Puck and Caliban
    In one explosive jest are blent.
    The boatmen on the river lent
An ear to hear the mirthful clan
    When Shakespeare laughed.

300TH ANNIVERSARY OF HERRICK'S
HESPERIDES

(1948)

I too, like Herrick, should at times
Ask pardon for "unbaptized rhymes."

Like Herrick, make apologies
For my own small *hesperides*.

Of course, like Herrick, I deplore them,
Ask nothing but oblivion for them.

Like Herrick, from my mind I swept them,
But,
    like Herrick,
                    always kept them.

ON A PORTRAIT OF
DR. SAMUEL JOHNSON, L.L.D.

(By Sir J. Reynolds, now owned by A.E.N.)

This is the Dr. Johnson of the "Prayers"—
    That great, tormented, craggy man, who poured
His sloth, his lovingkindness, and his cares
    In agonized petitions to the Lord.

O rough, pure, stubborn, troubled soul: for whom
    A smile of special tenderness men keep—
Who prayed for strength "to regulate my room,"
    And "preservation from immoderate sleep.". . .

If Life brought Dr. Johnson to his knees
It may bring others also, if you please—
Bachelors of Arts . . .
                    And L.L.D.'s.

66

DOROTHY

*"I made pies in the morning. William went
into the wood, and altered his poems."*—
Dorothy Wordsworth, July 28, 1800.

William went into the wood: the poem needed revising
  (Probably he put back what she had suggested first)
Dorothy watched the oven to see that the loaf was rising,
  Copied some Chaucer for him, and cooked and sewed
  and nursed.

William was out of spirits; Coleridge tramped from Kes-
  wick
  (Said his bowels were bad, and the wind made his eyes
  so sore)
Dorothy read their poems aloud, and gave them physic,
  Quitted her well-earned bed, and slept on the parlor
  floor.

She wept (she had her reasons); William said she "blub-
  bered";
  She walked the road to Rydal to see if the post went by;
William was reading Congreve, but Dorothy went to the
  cupboard
  And served the gooseberry pudding, and the homemade
  giblet pie.

William walked on the mountain; Dorothy planted broc-
  coli—

William could not "kindle," and had a pain in his head;
Coleridge had a fantod, but bore up well, and pluckily
  Let her broil him a mutton chop and serve it to him in
  bed.

Coleridge cut his name on stone, and Dorothy kissed the
  boulder;
  William danced with the daffodils, and took the word
  from her:
Then he rested, and had his nap leaning against her shoul-
  der—
  Only the very wise would guess whose poems they
  really were.

AUSTIN DOBSON

(1840–1921)
Austin Dobson, a writer of light verse.—
Newspaper obituary.

Ah! would that poets all could write
    In ink as clear as Dobson's was:
Master of airy fancy, light
    As morning cobwebs on the grass.

Tenderest trifles! how he caught
    (So charmingly, so many times)
The swift, reluctant birds of thought
    In the bright cages of his rhymes.

And Time, that jingles in his purse
    Mixed coinages, both new and old,
Makes change with bronze or silver verse
    But spends not his, a coin of gold!

INTERRUPTIONS

(an Essay in Verse)

Shakespeare, going good, in a working dream:—
    The cloudcapped towers, the gorgeous palaces,
    The solemn temples, the great globe itself,
    Yea—dissolve—inherit—
There comes a scream:
    Will, hither! Bestir thee, Will!
    (The man's a loon, I swear it)
    Dost naught about the house?
    Come to the aid of thy spouse,
    There's a mouse on the larder shelf
And the cat's upset the cream!

Happily combing his beard with an inky quill,
    Drinking port in seidels,
Tennyson deemed all else was nil
    But elegies and idylls:—
    Tears from the depth of some divine despair—
But from the top of the stair
Sounds the sudden scare, and shrill:
    Hurry up, Alf! Your Emily
    Is going to have more family;

Beat feet and do your share,
Tear up some old soft underwear,
Bring towels and hot water—
You've got another daughter.

Or Jefferson, on Independence bent:
We hold these truths self-evident—
Life—Liberty—unalienable right—
The patriot soul, in concentration whole,
Is making notes, for a thousand years of quotes—
Tom! You Tom! yells feminine lament;
And then, in a fit of the vapors:
Leave off those silly old papers,
The dogs are in a fight.

Maybe Goethe, steaming on his *Faust*
In a comfortable frowst,
In the twentieth year on the Second Part
Coming near the dream of his heart
Heard someone open the door, and roar:
Wolf! Gottes Willen, oeffnet das Fenster!
Lass fliegen die Gespenster!
That passage was irretrievably loused,
And he always held it against her.

The great Professor Stubbs, at Christmas '73,
Writing the preface to his History
(A masterpiece of jurisprudence,
Forgotten by most but Oxford students)—
The worst cause has often been illustrated
With the most heroic virtue—
But his mind is dissipated
When he hears the children bawl
In the home in Kettel Hall:—

The goose is on the table and we're starving;
Hi, Daddy! Regius Prof.!
It's time for scoff,
Come and do the carving!

There is one horror makes all writers kin,
Drives them to stomach ulcers or to gin:
Interruption, their poor alibi
For not writing things that never die.
But even more ridiculous and sad,
Those who lived so sheltered that they never had
Domestic uproar, or a telephone call,
Were never heard of at all.

AMMONOOSUC

(1938)

There are two streams that bear the name,
One is the Wild and one the Tame;
And on an afternoon we came
    To the Wild Ammonoosuc.

We lay in stupor, sweating, prone
Upon a ledge of sunwarmed stone;
I could not rest for beauty shown
    Beside the Ammonoosuc:

The small pink flower on supple stalk,
The confidential water-talk
As you came down from Moosilauke
    O amber Ammonoosuc.

71

Unspeakable in rhyme or prose
That moving Now the spirit knows,
The flow that pauses, pause that flows
   So like the Ammonoosuc,

And I, who had escaped from men,
From How and Why and Where and When,
Cried: Take me, make me whole again,
   O blessed Ammonoosuc.

Where her crystal overran it
I lay down in channeled granite;
Braced against the pushing planet
   I bathed in Ammonoosuc.

In that sluice of stream and sun
I dreamed that I and everyone
A whole new ethic had begun
   Inspired by Ammonoosuc.

Refreshed in her, I understand
One truth from A to ampersand:
That every heart in every land
   Has its own Ammonoosuc.

Be then, O secret cataract,
For me both parable and fact;
You gave me what my courage lacked
   O reckless Ammonoosuc.

When all the world moves widdershin
(Half Tory and half Jacobin)

Come pour your mountain freshet in
  My sweet Wild Ammonoosuc.

The open way has symbols three:
The fire, the stream, the growing tree;
If I grow morbid, say to me:
  Remember Ammonoosuc.

BALLAD OF NEW YORK, NEW YORK

Around the bend of Harbor Hill
  Comes Number 33,
Says: Board the cars, my bonny boy,
  And ride to Town with me.

A Town that has no ceiling price,
  A Town of double-talk;
A Town so big men name her twice,
  Like so: N'Yawk, N'Yawk.

Then spake the old Belittlin' Witch:
  "Beware the crowded trains;
Of all towns she's the Biggest Bitch—
  Bide here, and save your brains.

"What though she numbers boroughs five
  With many a noble spot,
Her thought is mostly gin and jive,
  Her repartee, So What?"

Himself replied: "Old Gloomy Spook,
   I fear no blatherskites,
I'll blow my nickle in the juke
   Behind the neon lights.

"Or I might even show 'em
   At Sardi's or The Stork—
I feel to write a poem
   About New York, New York."

The Witch:—

She's Run-around, and In-and-Out,
   And futile To-and-Fro,
And then what it was All About
   You will not even know.

She'll ring you mad by telephone
   And foul your wits with ink;
Men's tricks to get their product shown
   I will not say. They stink.

Across the fifty nations
   Her yokel accents go,
Her mispronunciations
   Broadcast by radio.

When ever did New York requite
   The glamor poets lent her?
Her soul is café-socialite,
   A simian garment-center.

Himself:—

The Town is what you make it
  Of glory and of pain;
I've earned the right to take it
  As Comédie Humaine.

For I have watched her faces
  To educate my soul,
Been drunk in public places
  With bliss, not alcohol.

Yes, I have known a crosstown street
  In sunset parallel
Where lovers lay in peace so sweet
  They never heard the El.

And I have stood, alone, alone,
  Where ships blew hoarse for sea
And armored planes were crowded on
  Like blackbirds on a tree.

The worm is on her portal?
  The Dollar is her joss?
Her sin is, being mortal?
  I enter: *Nolle Pros.*

The Witch:—

Okay. Then learn the answers,
  Eternally crack wise,
And be among the dancers
  With belladonna eyes.

75

Okay. All doors cry Welcome
  (If only Name you bring)
To swamis who talk talcum
  Or poets who can't sing.

Okay. Her mind still plays with blocks,
  And, reckoned in brain-hours,
When she outgrows her bobbysocks
  She starts on whiskey sours.

O consommé of gas-balloons,
  Whoopsdearie of them all!
A town of seven million goons
  Behind the octave ball.

Of what avail her towers high
  If in them men devote
Their minds to trivial things? But I
  Should worry! (End of quote.)

Himself:—

Avaunt, old bag! (Himself replied)
  Pipe down, and cut the squawk.
Your remarks are much too snide
  About N'Yawk, N'Yawk.

You bet, her tastes are corny:
  The public's always are;
And I may end my journey
  In some unritzy bar,

76

But, in the final ember,
    Discriminate am I;
From boyhood I remember
    Diana in the sky,

When life was all for learning
    (The top of human time!)
And mind was full of morning,
    And language burst with rhyme.

Now, when my hours are shortened,
    Fresh music I would bring;
She gives me, when disheartened,
    Magnificence to sing—

The song of smart connivers,
    Of crowded subway stops,
Of tough old taxi-drivers
    And much-enduring cops,

The ancient Down Town Fever,
    The smell of ferry slips,
And always and forever
    The pageant of her ships.

Unroll me then this mappamond
    Of all the life men know,
Grotesque and arabesque beyond
    The Tales of Edgar Poe.

And though she tear my mind in two
    In joy and pity split,

I love her; and so Nuts to You—
  It's *my* mind, isn't it?

New York, New York!—Two moods betwixt,
  Half fearful and half fain
(O love, O anger, always mixed!)
  He got aboard the train.

PEDOMETER

My thoughts beat out in sonnets while I walk,
And every evening on the homeward street
I find the rhythm of my marching feet
Throbs into verses (though the rhyme may balk.)
I think the sonneteers were walking men:
The form is dour and rigid, like a clamp,
But with the swing of legs the tramp, tramp, tramp
Of syllables begins to thud, and then—
Lo! While you seek a rhyme for *hook* or *crook*
Vanished your shabby coat, and you are kith
To all great walk-and-singers—Meredith,
And Shakespeare, Wordsworth, Keats, and Rupert Brooke!
Free verse is poor for walking, but a sonnet—
O marvellous to stride and brood upon it!

ARS DURA

How many evenings, walking soberly
Along our street all dappled with rich sun,
I please myself with words, and happily
Time rhymes to footfalls, planning how they run;
And yet, when midnight comes, and paper lies
Clean, white, receptive, all that one could ask,
Alas for drowsy spirit, weary eyes
And traitor hand that fails the well loved task!

Who ever learned the sonnet's bitter craft
But he had put away his sleep, his ease,
The wine he loved, the men with whom he laughed,
To brood upon such thankless tasks as these?
And yet, such joy does in that craft abide
He greets the paper as the groom the bride!

SIR KENELM

Now with a shout of joy I let you go:
Nothing, henceforward, can our triumphs vary;
We have been worthy of the moon and snow
And made long summer of our January.
Such tender incidence of chances odd
As saintlier lovers might have wished to die in
We've had; and also, O my God, my God,
What clear and cruel dusks to say good-by in.

And when we're old—if ever we *are* old—
And miracles once secretly impressed
Are evident on the brow for men to see,
There'll be some print there, subtle to behold,
Of all we knew and felt and learned and guessed
In days when I loved you, and you loved me.

CHATEAU DE MISSERY

"Here is a place where poems might be made.". . .
But in the linden arch such matins twittered,
Fish swam such curves beneath the balustrade,
The poet paused and found himself embittered.
Stubble was savoury by the grasscut edge,
The sun descanted Meursault-coloured shine,
And shamed by random mosses on the ledge
He corked the inkpot and uncorked the wine.

Here every shape outrhymes the poet's wit:
In every view such harmonies are spoken
New-joinered verses will not do, he fears.
Bring out some strong old sonnet, polished fit,
Plain as these grainy panels, dark and oaken,
Rubbed and sweetened by Burgundian years.

SONNET ON COPYRIGHT

(For Melville Cane and Max Chopnick)

There were two kinds of sonnets: *Whenas I,*
Or *As One Who*; and both were egotism;
But I should hope to write one, full and bye,
In the lighter colors of the prism.

I love them all, from Ronsard to Rossetti,
So syllabled in sable for the sibyl,
But mine, if I may toss my own confetti,
Will be at least, I pray, intelligible.

Of course it must have ambience of its own
(The critic-word in fashion nowadays)
But leave its foot and vestige on the stone
Like that Euclidean sandal of Millay's.

And it will be, or else the law is nix,
Copyright, until 2-0-0-6.

SONNET IN A KNOTHOLE

We idled at our doings, heart and I.
We watched the puddle lose its glaze of frost,
Measured the April in a pale March sky
And saw the birch-tree root all newly mossed.

Filling our fingernails with spring, we raked
And burned and swept, and breathed, and chopped some
    wood;
And even in that easiness, heart ached
To keep this noon forever, if we could.

But no one guessed (we made no outward stopping)
The sudden woodsman stroke that we incurred
When down through fiber, grain, and knotted wit
The oak of language shivered, cleanly split
By the flashed ax-blade of the perfect word.

We tightened steel to helve, and went on chopping.

OH TO BE IN "BARTLETT"
NOW THAT APRIL'S HERE

Today belongs in *Bartlett*! If men voted
For changeable sky, and air like cellophane,
Today would be a sonnet often quoted—
A sunny octave, a sestet of rain.
I went to that great Index, where I numbered
36 Mays; April scores 29;
Might not Today be added and remembered?
A footnote, or a single lingering line?

O April, month of malady and music!
One more would give one quote for every day,
So I reckoned. With a horrible phthisic
I mumbled hoarsely. In the tub I lay
Deep in hot water, steaming to the gills,
And thinking of my frozen daffodils.

82

END OF AUGUST

How gradual, gradual the dark came on:
If ever there were silence, that was it.
My freshcut grass smelled sweet as cinnamon,
I felt myself beginning to forget.
Almost equal in such dim desire
Were things I never won and things I lost
Till, chattering voltage like a broken wire
The wild cicada cried, Six weeks to frost!

Then dark was damnable. Night was too clear:
The trees no shelter, for the stars burned through;
And now this morning, when I first go out
What do I see, poised in the western sheer?
Curved downward like a hooked and leaping trout,
Waning, the moon we had when it was new.

THE WATCHMAN'S SONNET*

The night was heavy: thunder in suspense.
The shelves were gloom wherever one might look—
No darkness anywhere is quite so dense
As that shut up in a forgotten book.
Even the watchman at the timeclock desk
(Imaginative in his own despite)
Saw wisdom as a wavering grotesque,
A cone of shadow barely tipped with light.

83

Since men learned print, no night is wholly black,
But dawn was torrent, and fog followed rain.
Sideways he saw a flash, a speeding thing—
Lightning? He startled for the thunder-crack,
Then knew what flickered past the window pane:
Daylight, replenished on a bird's wet wing.

* Written, by the "Honorary Night Watchman," for the 50th anniversary of the Columbia University Press.

SHAKESPEARE IN JUNIOR HIGH

I'm reading Shakespeare, Fourteen Years confessed:
He's tops! I don't suppose in Junior High
We get it all: but gee, I like him best
When he writes about Me. He makes me cry!
Could I say that, in my English test?

Say it; and you, musicians of the spheres,
Know that your glory never was so great
As when our humble parallel appears,
And in the Universal agony
You recognize, condone, and sublimate
The all-devouring all-transmuting Me.

Bespeak us when we were savage, young, and pure:
When we lived, not studied, literature:
Sonnets not fourteen lines, but fourteen years.

ALEXANDER POPE, 1688–1744

POPE, who loved his rhymes in duplicates,
Chose couplets also for his mortal dates:
Born '88, precisian to the core,
Died, of exactitude, in '44.

Duplex himself, both wasp and honey-bee:
The wasp whose sting was immortality;
The bee whose nectar, sugared in the cyst,
Could turn to fury in a paper nest.

When Pope lit on the bare hide of a dunce
He did not need to do so more than once.
It was no use to rub the place in soap.
The only lucky fools were born since Pope.

Most perfect mind in English, he had fun:
Assassin and embalmer, both in one.

IN AN AUCTION ROOM

(Letter of John Keats to Fanny Brawne,
Anderson Galleries, March 15, 1920)
(To Dr. A. S. W. Rosenbach)

How about this lot? said the auctioneer;
One hundred, may I say, just for a start?

Between the plum-red curtains, drawn apart,
A written sheet was held. . . . And strange to hear
(Dealer, would I were steadfast as thou art)
The cold quick bids. *(Against you in the rear!)*
The crimson salon, in a glow more clear
Burned bloodlike purple as the poet's heart.

Song that outgrew the singer! Bitter Love
That broke the proud hot heart it held in thrall—
Poor script, where still those tragic passions move—
Eight hundred bid: fair warning: the last call:
The soul of Adonais, like a star. . . .
Sold for eight hundred dollars—Doctor R.!

CHARLES AND MARY

(December 27, 1834)

*Lamb died just before I left town, and Mr. Ryle of the
E. India House, one of his extors., notified it to me. . . . He
said Miss L. was resigned and composed at the event, but
it was from her malady, then in mild type, so that when
she saw her brother dead, she observed on his beauty
when asleep and apprehended nothing further.*—Letter of
John Rickman, 24 January, 1835.

I hear their voices still: the stammering one
Struggling with some absurdity of jest;
Her quiet words that puzzle and protest
Against the latest outrage of his fun.

So wise, so simple—has she never guessed
That through his laughter, love and terror run?
For when her trouble came, and darkness pressed,
He smiled, and fought her madness with a pun.

Through all those years it was his task to keep
Her gentle heart serenely mystified.
If Fate's an artist, this should be his pride—
When, in that Christmas season, he lay dead,
She innocently looked. "I always said
That Charles is really handsome when asleep."

ELECTED SILENCE: THREE SONNETS

(In loving memory of William Rose Benét, 1886–1950)

I

This was my song, unsingable, unsung;
Long put aside in grieving or in sloth:
Such heaviness to raise the simple word
(How well we knew, is likeliest unheard)
The brain, the good gray dishclout, to be wrung.
Brain split? Fatigue, or indolence, or both?
But mute in midnight now, forgotten man
(No phone will ring) his memory might plan.
Yet (as you said) I was at whiles too clever
In selfish craft and curious fashioning:
Oh why, why did I ever
Do anything but sing?

II

Our time was late for singing, blessed Bill!
We sang: we reeled our purple *qwertyuiop*
As our gaffers would have pared a quill,
Took *fin-de-siècle* by the forward top.
Did sidekick duty in our Grub-street shop
And ribbed each other plenty. You might say
Something of mine was corn and sugar-pop—
I cracked, *You* should know, William Prose Benét.
We laughed, and loved us more. Too late for song?
Sure, singing hath no age? Tremble lives long.
I spoke you always as my Wilhelm Meister,
Shy, and shyer yet, but never shyster.
What 1900 japes and *bouts rimés*
We had: but we were singing all the way.

III

So . . . so . . . each poet has his secret faith
That somewhen, somewhen, someone might arise,
Might read him with unfashionable eyes,
Critic uncrazed by momentary scathe,
So skilled in loves or laughters and/or lust
Dissects the formal flaky pastrycrust
To our god-orchard deepdish fruit below . . .
And now no postage-stamp will let you know.
We saw men in their universal blitz
Tear our bicycle-boyhood world to bits,
Yet also saw tree, ocean surf, and hill
In the morn's morning measured fresh and new.
My faith, such as it is (not much), dear Bill
Is partly faith in you.

INVOCATION TO AN AUDIENCE

Now for the moment are your minds removed
From everything but loveliness,
And you here present, if you've ever loved,
Loved and then wearied of that sweet distress,
You who have dearly proved
The arrow's sharpness and the archer's blindness
Remember still, as best behooved,
His lovingkindness.

TOULEMONDE DESIPIENT

In this life so slippery
Dulce est desipere.
What are the joys of men?
Enumerate them, then.
Ink that runs from the pen
And forms unbidden the desiderate word;
Scraps of conversation overheard;
Swimming after sweat;
Driving a car;
Remembering the name of one unexpectedly met;
The first cocktail at the bar.
The first warm sun in March;
Collars without starch;
Finding a rare edition;
The dawning dim suspicion
That dame likes me: I think we might go far.

Making a full house from a pair;
Switching comedians off the air.
Among the pleasures particularly man's
Are: mushroom soup in cans;
Old brown shoes well shined;
The laughter hidden in the mind;
Days when everything seems funny;
The return of long-loaned money;
Full appreciation of some art
(Whether hockey or Hokusai);
A bad cold nursed with rock-and-rye;
Hitching the horse behind the cart;
Believing in your soul
The part is greater than the whole.
The joy of being warm
By firelight on a night of storm;
Moonlight when it stipples
Long Island Sound in ripples.

The footlights glowing on the curtain
On a First Night of your own;
Remembering, though uncertain,
A number on the phone;
Books on which there's a hoodoo
Because no one likes them as well as you do,
Or very few do.

The fun that people miss
By being prim and priss
(Also the snags they strike
By doing too much what they like);
Morning papers and orange juice on breakfast tables;
The almost vanished smell of livery stables;

Engines that go by steam
(For pistons and cranks,
Oh Lord, my thanks);
The curiosities of dream;
An unexpected Valentine;
Spaghetti and red wine.
Hot towels at the barber's;
Tea and bread-and-butter in English arbors;
Falling asleep with a detective story
(One that's both intelligent and gory).

The feeling of a day when nothing has to be done:
No appointments, absolutely none,
Just to loiter along the shelves
Reintegrating all one's various selves;
And then, when everyone's in bed,
The silence overhead.

His blue morocco slippers donned,
What evenings then had Toulemonde.

IT WILL LAST MY TIME

I tried my mind to quiet
  With verses mixed or plain,
But now that I have nothing
  For losing, or for gain,
I whisper you my secret,
  My private gin-and-lime—
  It will last my time.

They tell me space collapses
    Till rockets travel soon
By planet-platforms mooring
    For journeys to the moon.
I've done my share of roaming
    By wheel and keel and climb—
    It will last my time.

New verses shall be written
    (I hear) in braver mode,
And no one dreams attempting
    The rondeau, or the ode:
I loved all kinds of poems,
    Some even were in rhyme—
    It will last my time.

They say love will be richer,
    Fresh passions deeper move:
Bushwa! if I remember,
    Myself invented love!
Thank God, such wealth of loving
    I've had since early prime—
    It will last my time.

FOR A DAUGHTER'S WEDDING

I know so little, but have private music
    And ancient books, if needed, I can turn;
Myself must be both pharmacy and physic,
    However slow to learn.

O late indeed my heart grew knowledgeable:
  Snow on the sill and satire on the brow!
But habit can endure incorrigible—
  It does not matter now.

I thought I heard a voice cry out in sleeping,
  I paused, all father, listening up the stair,
The ancient, the instinctive vigil keeping—
  But there was no child there.

Old human cycle! where begun or ended
  No indignant sire has ever known—
Go you then, create, as is intended
  Your secrets all your own.

WINTER'S TALE

I was moody in pale December
Under the day's westfallen ember
Thinking verse of an older mode—
Verse like trees, black filigrees
In a sunset freeze, on a snowbound road.

Still proud to remember, on Dead-End Street,
I laughed from laughter that never after
My love has varied since first and ago
As both we know my love I buried
In your innermost naked sweet.

Even in ice-glaze January
My loving or losing do not vary:

There is no changing nor estranging
The natural greed, the mortal passion,
The need that joins the unlocked loins.

I chose, on a road that froze, this verse;
Small silver for the purse, but coins
Of sterling in an older fashion.
That road, however they ice and snow it,
I never trod except as poet.
For all we loved, for all I lost,
This is silver, and melting frost.

MADRIGAL NOT TO BE REPRINTED

I, too, have tried to be modern.—W. B. Yeats (1935)

When your mood is joy
Give out with a shout, bully-boy:
Riotous, pink as a child from sleep,
Eyes burning Saxon-blue
Let the rabble share with you
And babble, and applaud it.
Laughter needs audit.

But if (it might be tomorrow)
You are despair,
Then secret keep; quiet creep
Into your sorrow.
There you live alone,
Breech and bone and marrow.
Retire, retreat, repair,
Immurable in your lair.

Defeat no company will bear,
No consort, hide nor hair,
Sorrow wants no one there,
Not anyone, anywhere.

TOO LONG I LOITERED

Too long I loitered in dismay
Where word-crammed silences divide
The heart from what it craves to say.
The snow was caked northside the tree
And I was bored to death with Me.
I had no song, I had no pride,
And growing old, and terrified.

Then late of more than sixty springs
Came plain language unforeboded,
Speech that needed no rehearse:
Just in time the curse exploded,
Shattered black imaginings,
And music canceled in one verse
A million hours of trivial things.

AND A CROOKED TREE

An evening star, and a crooked tree
Are clarified on dusk for me;
And I, who have scarce energy
My private verse to copy fair,
Am frost-consumed in vesper air.

But what of the world and I not there?
Do I really care?
I had good advice for men's despair:
You can find it exactly where
I said it. Most of it's o.p.*

Yes, I shall miss you terribly,
My evening star and my crooked tree,
When Orion, isosceles, angled right,
Comes tilting northward through the night.

* Out of print.

TO HIS EXECUTORS

They tried to make guesses
    What I held most dear—
For instance, addresses
    Copied year by year.
They were quick to discover
    With knowing look
What was carried over
    To each New Year's book.

Some made them smile, some made them frown;
    But, literal-minded, they never guessed—
You don't need to write down
    What you love best.

NIGHTSONG OF LORD CULVERIN ON THE DRAWBRIDGE OF CASTLE QUERULOUS

Sing sotto voce. Don't embellish.
Who one else would ever relish
What I found heavenly or hellish?

The cheesecurve moon, flotilla-high,
Focussed with one mudshot eye
After one drink too much of rye.

The roses, in the dusk grown duller,
Drain their pinks and reds of color.

Comes dark, more genitive and sadder,
Pernoctate by my two-hour bladder,

When, bundled on my truss of hay,
I pray to think, and think to pray.

My poor fantastical routine
By no one else, thank God, is seen.

No one other dares to guess
The rites to which my heart cried Yes!

They were the selfishness of me?
I was myself, I had to be.

Quit waxing, moon; quit sweetening, shrubs—
Quit pointing at me, maiden bubs.

Soft airs, wing-beetles, crowd about!
Good night, my lovers. My lamp is out.

II

TRANSLATIONS FROM THE CHINESE

THE PALIMPSEST

There is, in each man's heart,
Chinese writing—
A secret script, a cryptic language:
The strange ideographs of the spirit,
Scribbled over or half erased
By the swift stenography of daily life.

No man can easily decipher this cordiscript,
This blurred text corrupted by fears and follies;
But now and then,
Reading his own heart
(So little studied, such fine reading matter!)
He sees fragments of rubric shine through—
Old words of truth and trouble
Illuminated, red and gold.
The study of this hidden language
Is what I call
Translating from the Chinese.

INSCRIPTION FOR A BUTTERFLY'S WING

There are two Languages:
One is of Great Mandarins and Important Affairs,
It is civil, precise, and meaningless.

The other,
The Speech of the Spirit,
So rarely spoken, so dimly understood,
Is haltingly whispered
By lonely men.
In the first I am glib,
In the latter I stammer;
But I know which will serve me
In the Foreign Land.

TESTAMENT OF NO SHO

Prithee (cried No Sho, the young poet)
Shut out the baby:
Don't let her come into my thinking-room.
She is a darling
And her every movement is a loveliness;
But how can I afford to look at her—
I, who already have notes for hundreds more poems
Than I can ever write.

For I have had moments
When every form and color of life
Seemed bursting with naked poetry—
> *Broadway for the taxis,*
> *Columbus for the L,*
> *But Amsterdam's the Avenue*
> *Where trucks go down like hell—*

And there are so many lovely poems being written
I am amazed:

For how do the darling poets find time and chance to live
        them,
Those moments of millennium
When the mind ignites the hand?
But for this was I born
And for this came I into the world
To blow from the slippery suds of life
My bubbles of fragile glee.

THE CIGARETTE STUB

Tossed aside in the uproar
No Sho was quenched;
But in his verses
You will hear a satirical whisper
Like the hiss of a cigarette stub
Cast into a sink.

OF A POET WHO DIED YOUNG

He was master of the stop-short,
Brief poems in which the words are few
But the meaning continues in readers' hearts.
His life, too, was like that.

STOP-SHORT

All poems, in all tongues, in all ages,
Say always the same thing:
Here am I, darling,
But where art thou?

POETS EASILY CONSOLED

The anguishes of poets are
Less grim than other men's, by far:
When other men can only curse,
The poet puts his woes in verse.
And Yee Lee, though at first the pang was smart
When by his friend Wu Wu his bride was stolen,
Soon asked which best expressed a broken heart,
A dash, a comma, or a semi-colon?

AN ARISTOCRAT OF THE P'UN DYNASTY

Just as the beheading was all ready to begin,
"What was *your* offense?" they asked the ancient man-
   darin.
The mandarin smiled grimly, as on his knees he sank.
"My offense?" he whispered: "Ah, my offense is—rank."

EVASIONS

The Old Mandarin is pure in heart
But he understands the necessities of Policy.
When the doctors examined him for life insurance
They asked him if he ever drank
Alcoholic liquors;
To which he answered "In moderation."
They urged him to be more definite.
"What do you mean," they said, "by moderate?
Do you mean just about Average?"
He had no idea what would be considered Average
In a Prohibition country,
But knew they'd certainly be scandalized
By a Chinese philosopher's idea of Moderation.
He was wary in reply,
But when they said "Have you ever been intoxicated?"
He remarked nobly
"Sirs, I am a Poet."

UNFASHIONABLE

Poets in our civilization must be difficult.—T. S. Eliot, 1921.

> In hope to please futurity,
> Win critical security,
> I strove to write obscurity,
>   Said the Old Mandarin.

In spite of all acidity,
Humidity, morbidity,
Alas for me, lucidity
    Was always breaking in.

CHINESE BARTLETT

They asked the Old Mandarin:
Why don't you write a real book,
Something with less promiscuity
And more continuity?

He replied: What remains of any book
After a little while
But a few quotes and excerpts?
A few half-rememberables
More than half-forgotten.*
Why not just write the excerpts
To begin with?

* Half-remembered is not the same
  As half-forgotten.
  The half we remembered
  Is *ours*.

IRREVERENCE

Listen! (exclaimed the guests,
Taking tea in the next room)
Listen to the Old Mandarin's typewriter!
He must be going good.

Cumquats, said Poo Pitty Sing.
When he goes as fast as that
He's only X-ing out.

BRIEF BIOGRAPHIES

I

He was a delicious companion
Said Lady Lotus:
He was thoughtful not to say
Things Better Unsaid,
But he always wrote them to me afterward
When I could really enjoy them.

II

Some people said
He was at his best when alone
But he was never like that
When I was with him.

CLASS DISMISSED

One of his lovely pupils
Studying Chinese classics
Said, "It occurs to me,
What is the feminine for *Mandarin?*"

"It occurs to me,"
Said the Old Mandarin gallantly,
"*You* are."

LOW MEMORABILITY

What sort of a day, O.M.?

Wonderful!
I thought of the absolutely right word
For one of my little sayings.
So right that no one
Will ever notice it.

Good old rainbow-chaser!
What was it?

Sacro-iliac! . . . I've forgotten.

DIM VIEW

"I've been reading," said Poo Pitty Sing,
"The *Journal to Stella.*
Gosh, what letters
The Dean did write her;
But I take rather
A dim view of Stella:
What did she have
That I haven't got?"

She had Jonathan Swift.

PRAGMATISM

When Chancellor Mu Kow and I were ennuyés
We used to go to the windy hill
And fly paper kites.
"Have you considered, Tremendous One"
(I asked him),
"The paradox of the kite?
To make it soar steadily
You must weight it down with a tail;
And to keep the spirit lofty, it is well . . ."
—"Do not, I beg you"
(Replied the Great Magistrate),
"Unsettle me with analogies,
You have only to meditate and watch the goldfish,
I must govern a province."

NONE OF MY BUSINESS

I saw a satisfied bee
Blissfully asleep in a hollyhock flower.
I tickled him with a straw
To see if he would wake,
And then I was ashamed
Realizing how gravely I had been infected
By your American passion for interfering
In other people's affairs.
No harm was done, however—
He only grumbled affectionately
And turned over on the other side.

CHINESE ACTOR

My favorite actor is the one
Whose name I see
So frequently
On the marquee:
Sat Sun Mon.

SALTIMBANQUE

All round the margin
Of any consignment of print
Is a continuous flicker of readers
Leaping to Conclusions—
Excellent conclusions for them, no doubt,
But not necessarily the author's.

INSCRIPTION FOR A BOILED SHIRT

Truth
Is often uncouth.

A lie, for politesse,
Wears evening dress
And with all its faults
Is graceful as a waltz.

HEGELIAN ANTITHESIS

When, as a child, I noticed
That coal and ice were always sold
By the same merchant
I first suspected
The irremediable duplicity of the world.

111

THE HUBBUB OF THE UNIVERSE

Man makes a great fuss
About this planet
Which is only a ball-bearing
In the hub of the universe.
It reminds me
Of the staff of a humorous weekly
Sitting in grave conference
On a two-line joke.

HANDICAPPED

Life is a game of whist
Between Man and Nature
In which Nature knows all Man's cards.
Well, suppose I try you out on trumps,
Says Nature,
Leading the mating instinct.

QUERY

Who can alleviate
The joy of a social worker
Alleviating
The sorrows of the poor?

112

DIAL CALL

Deep calleth unto deep
(Said Psalm 42, vii)
But also shallow unto shallow
And gets more prompt reply.

WEAKNESS

If you approach me
I shall cheerfully promise
More than I can perform:
For I have my frailties.

But withinward, my soul
Evades, eludes, recedes;
And you must not be peevish—
I have my own secrets to pursue.
And so have you.

THE SURF

We took the baby
(Three years old)
To the beach at Lloyd's Neck.

113

A cold northern day and the wind was crisping
    surf on the beach.
She looked at the white foam
And heard its rhyming prosody.
"Snow," she announced.
"Snow saying, Sorrow to come in,
Sorrow to come in."

TO C.H.P.

Cross-legged in pyjamas on the floor at one A.M.
Under an electric light
I was enjoying some Japanese poetry.
Suddenly the light went out:
Through the tracery of the oak tree
I saw the old moon rising,
One burning star balanced in a cool chink,
Heard the steady thrill of the crickets—
A hokku, a very hokku!
There, unguessed and unregarded
Had been the perfect essence of what I was admiring
In mere paper and ink.
This is very important, I said,
As I stared at the fragile night.
The bulb went out on purpose to teach me
Not to take the translation for the original.

THE NEW MOON FEELING

How is it, by what incalculable instinct,
That now and then, in a clean afternoon,
By some touch of air or slope of twilight,
Without previous thought I say to myself
(And am unerringly right)
It feels as if
There were a New Moon.

VIGILIAE ALBAE

Now I am silent and my name is Tacitus.
But in this douce brightness
I have to pause now and then
Putting the moon behind the pine tree
To give myself respite
From her cruel and insinuating lustre.
O moon, scratch-pad of poets,
More meant against than meaning!

THE POINT OF VIEW

When the birch tree was cut down
The birds came and sat on the trunk
And gossiped.

In this tree I found the largest caterpillar I ever ate,
Said the robin.
In this tree I met my first wife,
Said the wren.

LOST, LOST

The last Saturday night in September
Said an American authority
We return to Standard Time
And regain the hour we lost last April,
Thus evening up.

Dear boy, how fallacious is the equation.
Since when was an hour of September sleeping
Worth sixty minutes of April midnight?
Autumn gives noble and brilliant pangs,
But never an equivalent
Of what we lost in spring.

Autumn is an essayist,
But Spring was a poet.

NOTE FOR A BRITISH TRAVELER

Across our flat Long Island shires
You need not look for huntsman squires.
That barking is not hounds or harriers,
But caused by (*Yoicks!*) hay-fever carriers.

SEED ON THE WIND

On a day of keen October
The city was filled with floating seeds,
Tiny fluffs of milkweed or cat-tail
Blown from Hackensack meadows
Where autumn is something more
Than a forest of stone perpendiculars.
And all day long
On busy street crossings
Men reached to grasp the drifting gauzes
With twinges they couldn't explain.

MANHATTAN

These many years, said the commuter, hibernating
      in town,
She was a mistress I never truly embraced:
I only kissed her hand and said good-bye at dusk.
Now we lie together.
She holds me deep in her strong bosom.
All night long I hear her breathe and murmur.
Sometimes she talks in my sleep.

MISTAKE

I woke drowsily in the night
And heard a rush of cars.
Country ears, quicker than reason,
Thought: what a wind has risen
Among my tall strong trees.

BOOKS IN THE DARK

Suddenly I thought of all my books
Locked up in a house in the country.
Darkness and cold creep in
Between the bravest pages.
Do you miss the lamplight, William Hazlitt?
Do you remember me at all, John Donne?

STERN CHASE

Sometimes, watching the electric news bulletin
In Times Square,
I forget to read the fiery message
Fascinated to watch the little flickering period
Swimming along at the tail of the sentence
Like a baby goldfish
Trying to catch up.
I have a horrid thought, that's Me.

SOFT SHOULDER ON FIFTH AVENUE

Confectioners—for instance Schrafft's—
Have the pleasantest of crafts.

Each sweet the candy-merchant wraps
In little crimpy cups. . . . Perhaps

My greedy love likewise belongs
In fluted papers—only songs.

There used to be little golden tongs.

WHEN YOU'RE WRITING

Remember, when you're writing about New York,
Faces are as important as buildings.

Dive deep into the subway, that gallery of portraiture;
Bathe your eyes in that flood of bitter truth.
It is not lovely, it proves no theorems,
But there is no weariness it cannot heal.

Generalizers on human trouble,
Have you courage to face those faces?
You, and you, and you, seen only once,
Good-bye forever, and good luck.

119

VERY FEW REMEMBER

As I went down from Trenton
By a strip of canal sword-blade blue in the dusk,
I suddenly remembered
That this was the way to Camp Dix
And I remembered
Troop trains travelling in the night.

FEBRUARY FILLDYKE

Snow is beautiful
But there can be too much of it
And the ancient Chinese poets
Who praised it in crystal verses
Never had to drive a car
On icy roads.
But still, enduringly romantic
I maintain that snow
Makes brick steps wonderfully pink
When you sweep them.

IGNITION

When you think of a thing
(Said a poet, tall with glory,
Which is very good for poets)
The work is over.
I know what he meant. . . .
I wish it were so.

A CASUAL THOUGHT

Just by accident, I suppose,
I am thinking of the world's unpublished poems
And the beautiful imperative reasons
For not publishing them.

QUERY

If every other poet
Means as much more than he says in his verses
As I do in mine
How shall I read poetry intelligently?

BIVALVES

The pearl
Is a disease of the oyster.
A poem
Is a disease of the spirit
Caused by the irritation
Of a granule of Truth
Fallen into that soft gray bivalve
We call the mind.

"AUTHOR WILL SUPPLY"

The anxious author, when engaged
Correcting proof sheets newly paged
May find a memo of this sort
(The printer's warning): *One Line Short.*

And though I write this verse of mine
    To give your thought a moment's play,
The text is also short one line—
    And you know well what it would say.

BAUBLE FOR CRITICS

I am weary
Of critical theory.

I'm empiric
About a lyric.

Either it sings
Like a happy peasant,
Or—one of those things—
It just doesn't.

GRINDING TEETH

Nothing in the life of Lord Byron
Pleases me so much as the fact that his dentist
Said he was damaging his teeth
By grinding them in his sleep,
And I think how many Literary Critics
Are probably doing the same thing
This very night.

RECIPROCATION

One good nocturne
Deserves another,
Said George Sand
When she met Chopin.

LONELY FUN

Philologists
Have lonely fun all by themselves.
Sarcastic, for instance, means a flesh-eater
And it's wrong to apply it,
As the New York *Times* always does,
To Bernard Shaw.

G.B.S., 1856—

What obsequies for dear old Shaw
Who lived outside the canon law?
Let's give him, to be truly Shavian,
All rites, including Scandinavian.

PHILOLOGIST AT THE TRAIN GATE

Have they no vowels of compassion?
  By some Grimm Law they always say
In their peculiar diphthong fashion:
  All abard for Erster Bay!

This idiosyncrasy should teach
Some new phonetic law of speech,
But never mind linguistic turns—
We'll miss it! Hurry! *Goid your lerns!*

FALSE ALARM

I sit here tonight
Fortified in my own particular silence.
Donny, the sheep-dog, lies in the next room,
And sometimes, when he stirs,
The tinkle of his license tag
Seems, for the dreadful tithing of a second,
The preliminary tocsin of a telephone call.

In that bursting schism of the mind
My whole wary garrison leaps furious to defense
And my walls bristle with armored paladins
Ready with reasons why I shouldn't do
Whatever it is
Whoever might want.

ANGUISH IN HERBA

The friendly curious children
    Loquaciously come near:
The poet in his greenwood
    Lurks in angry fear.

There, his private thinking
    By innocence defiled,
More than hell or Hitler
    He fears the neighbor's child.

SEDUCED

Now comes after-lunch, the hour of dread.
The Baltimore oriole, Malvolio from Maryland,
Warbles his luscious lyric:
Why do you work, why?
Why? Why work?
There's a new detective story—

UNDERTONE

The very day I set aside for writing
The plumbers came unexpectedly.
I fear through all my verses
You may overhear the clang of pipes,
And voices in the cellar.

A LESSON

The path was strewn, one day last winter
With curly shards of clear ice,
Broken tubes of frozen rain
Blown from the trees.
I wanted to go out and study them again
To see exactly what they looked like,
But I didn't.
I try to teach myself,
We are given only one chance to see things.
We can't always go back for another look.

LEGACY

The year has made her will: she left to me
A private purse:
Silver and copper from the dogwood tree,
White gold from a torrent, amber from a pond,
And, for my sadness' sake,
Mountains in a bluescape of beyond.
It might be worse:
These will be useful when I lie awake.

PAYABLE ON DEMAND

What discount does the broker quote
    On loans we once held cheap?
I mean, Death's promissory note,
    A night of perfect sleep.

TWO THINGS

Two things are troublesome to me
    And turn my warm blood cold:
The briefness of the dogwood tree,
The knowledge that there still will be
    Full moons when I am old.

128

Then passively I realize
(With some surprise)
I would not have it otherwise.

GEMMATION IN NOVEMBER

Like trees and shrubs,
I have a false budding
In warm Indian Summer.
Windfall wood in the fireplace
Burns a sweet peppery smell.

ULTIMATUM

Student of the Neverlasting Now
I know too well, necessity inveterate
Corrupts my vivid Present into Preterite.

O ultimate verb, so variously inflected,
Be unexpected:
As you Say When, allow
Just time for my Here's How.

PREFACE TO BARTLETT

In poetry there is one test of art:
With whispering stealth, and keeping delicate time,
It creeps into your mind; you find it there.
You are my poem, then, for in my heart
Lovelier than a sonnet you made rhyme
And I had memorized you unaware.

APPENDIX: ORDER OF PUBLICATION

I

POEMS

from *The Eighth Sin* (Oxford, Blackwell, 1912)
Twilight
from *Songs For A Little House* (New York, Doran, 1917)
Washing The Dishes
Pedometer
Ars Dura
A Grub Street Recessional
from *The Rocking Horse* (New York, Doran, 1919)
When Shakespeare Laughed
from *Hide And Seek* (New York, Doran, 1920)
To His Mistress, Deploring That He Is Not An Elizabethan Galaxy
Nursery Rhymes For The Tender-Hearted: I
In An Auction Room
from *Chimneysmoke* (New York, Doran, 1921)
At The Mermaid Cafeteria
Charles And Mary
The Poet On The Hearth
from *Where The Blue Begins* (New York, Doubleday, Page, 1922)
Where The Blue Begins

132

133

TRANSLATIONS FROM THE CHINESE

135

SELECTED BIBLIOGRAPHY

The Eighth Sin. Oxford, B. H. Blackwell, 1912.
  Morley's first book.
Songs For A Little House. New York, George H. Doran, 1917.
The Rocking Horse. New York, George H. Doran, 1919.
  First appearance of the "translations from the Chinese,"
  under the title "Synthetic Poems."
Hide And Seek. New York, George H. Doran, 1920.
Chimneysmoke. New York, George H. Doran, 1921.
Translations From The Chinese. New York, George H. Doran,
  1922.
Where The Blue Begins. New York, Doubleday, Page, 1922.
  A novel.
Parsons' Pleasure. New York, George H. Doran, 1923.
The Haverford Edition. New York, Doubleday, Page, 1927.
  The twelve volume collected edition; Volume VII is "Poems
  and Translations From The Chinese."
Translations From The Chinese. New York, Doubleday, Page,
  1927. An enlarged edition.
Toulemonde. New York, Doubleday, Doran, 1928.
Poems. New York, Doubleday, Doran, 1929.
John Mistletoe. New York, Doubleday, Doran, 1931.
  Morley's early autobiography.
Mandarin In Manhattan. New York, Doubleday, Doran, 1933.
Streamlines. New York, Doubleday, Doran, 1936.
  Essays, with a section of "translations from the Chinese."

The Trojan Horse. Philadelphia, Lippincott, 1937.
A novel.

The Middle Kingdom, Poems, 1929–1944. New York, Harcourt, Brace, 1944.

Spirit Level And Other Poems. Cambridge, Harvard University Press, 1946.

The Old Mandarin, More Translations From The Chinese. New York, Harcourt, Brace, 1947.

Poetry Package. New York, Louis Greenfield, 1950.
Poems by Morley and William Rose Benét.

The Ballad Of New York, New York, And Other Poems, 1930–1950. New York, Doubleday, 1950.

Gentlemen's Relish. New York, W. W. Norton, 1955.
Morley's last book.